·ANIMALS ILLUSTRATED·

Bowhead Whale

Bowhead Whale

by **Joanasie Karpik** • illustrated by **Sho Uehara**

INHABIT

MEDIA

Published by Inhabit Media Inc.
www.inhabitmedia.com

Inhabit Media Inc. (Iqaluit), P.O. Box 11125, Iqaluit, Nunavut, X0A 1H0
(Toronto), 191 Eglinton Avenue East, Suite 301, Toronto, Ontario, M4P 1K1

Design and layout copyright © 2017 Inhabit Media Inc.
Text copyright © 2017 by Joanasie Karpik
Illustrations by Sho Uehara copyright © 2017 Inhabit Media Inc.

Editors: Neil Christopher, Kathleen Keenan
Art Director: Danny Christopher
Designer: Astrid Arijanto

We acknowledge the support of the Canada Council for the Arts for our publishing program.

This project was made possible in part by the Government of Canada.

ISBN: 978-1-77227-162-1

Printed in Canada

Library and Archives Canada Cataloguing in Publication

Karpik, Joanasie, author
Bowhead whale / by Joanasie Karpik ; illustrated by Sho Uehara.

(Animals illustrated)
ISBN 978-1-77227-162-1 (hardcover)

1. Bowhead whale--Juvenile literature. I. Uehara, Sho, illustrator
II. Title. III. Series: Animals illustrated

QL737.C423K37 2017   j599.5'276   C2017-907062-2

Canadä   Canada Council   Conseil des Arts
                for the Arts   du Canada

Table of Contents

The Bowhead Whale

The bowhead whale is a very large animal that lives in the Arctic Ocean. Like all whales, bowhead whales are mammals. They breathe air through the 2 blowholes on top of their head. Bowhead whales have huge heads that take up about one third of their entire body.

Bowhead whales are the second-largest animal in the world. Only the blue whale is bigger. Bowhead whales can weigh between 150,000 and 200,000 pounds (about 68,000 and 91,000 kilograms) and grow to between 50 and 60 feet (about 15 and 18 metres). They are usually black with white or grey patches on their lower jaws, bellies, and tails.

Let's learn more about bowhead whales!

Range

Bowhead whales are found in the Arctic Ocean. They are rarely seen south of the Arctic.

Bowhead whales live in the waters around Nunavut and north of the Yukon and the Northwest Territories. They are also found in the waters around Alaska and Greenland.

For most of the year, especially spring, many bowhead whales can be found around the edges of ice floes. In the summer, they swim farther north to find more food. People are most likely to see bowhead whales during the summer.

Skeleton

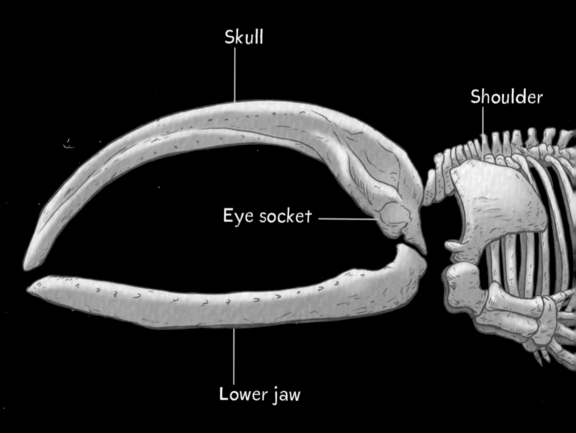

Skull

Shoulder

Eye socket

Lower jaw

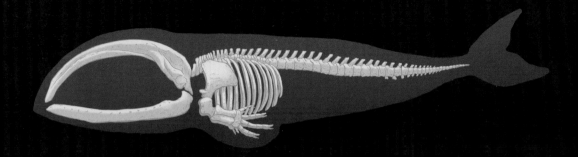

Tail

lipper

Blowholes

Bowhead whales use their blowholes to breathe by poking the tops of their heads out of the water.

When bowhead whales swim under the sea ice, they can use their heads to break breathing holes in the ice. Some bowhead whales have been seen breaking through ice up to 8 inches (about 20 centimetres) thick.

Baleen

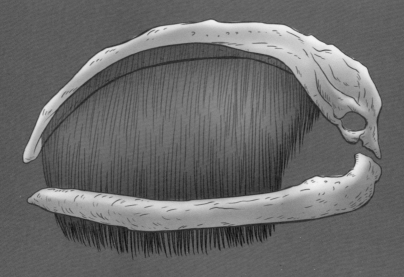

Baleen plates

Bowhead whales are part of a group of whales known as "baleen whales." Baleen whales do not have teeth. Instead, they have plates in their mouths called "baleen plates" that they use to trap food while they swim. These plates hang down from the whale's upper jaw.

A bowhead whale can have hundreds of baleen plates. Even though these plates look a little bit like hair, they are made from a material similar to human fingernails. This material is called "keratin."

Diet

Bowhead whales eat very small creatures called "zooplankton." Zooplankton are tiny animals that live in the ocean and drift along with the current. They are so small that human eyes cannot see them without a microscope. Inuit call these tiny animals "*illiraq.*"

When bowhead whales are hungry, they swim near the surface of the water with their mouths open. As they swim, their baleen plates trap zooplankton.

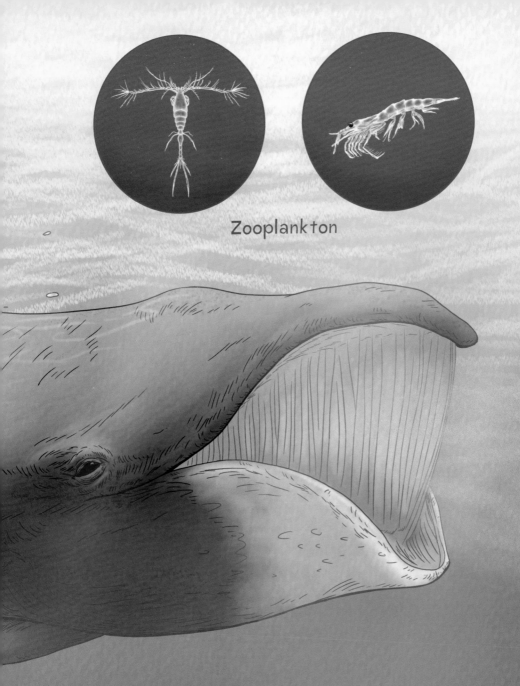

Zooplankton

A bowhead whale can eat about 4,000 pounds
(about 1,800 kilograms) of zooplankton in a day.

Babies

A baby bowhead whale is called a "calf." Bowhead whales have their babies in the spring. A female bowhead whale usually has a calf every 3 or 4 years.

Calves can swim soon after they are born, but they stay close to their mothers for almost a year so that they can drink their mothers' milk.

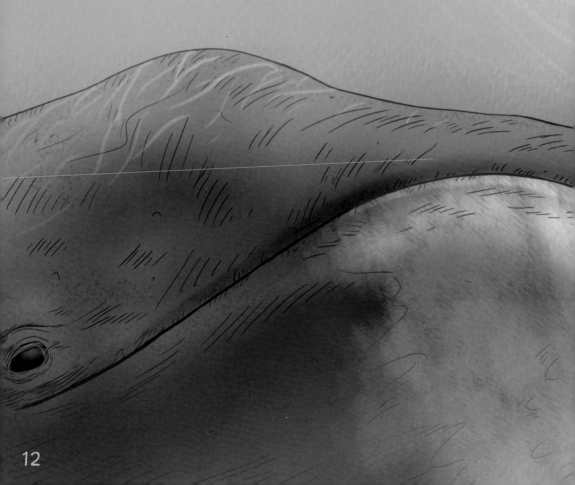

When they are born, calves are usually blue or grey. Their skin darkens as they get older.

Predators

Orca whales are the main predators of bowhead whales. "Predators" are the animals that try to catch and eat bowhead whales. When orcas are together in a group, called a "pod," they will attack a bowhead whale as a group.

Inuit have observed the oldest orca in the pod attacking the bowhead whale's tail while the other orcas attack the rest of its body. To escape the pod, the bowhead whale will try to swim toward land.

Communication

Unlike some other whales, bowhead whales are often found on their own. Sometimes they will travel in small groups to find food.

Although they are often seen swimming alone, bowhead whales use sound to communicate with each other. Mothers and calves have been heard making calls that sound like moans. When male bowhead whales are looking for mates, they make repeated calls to female whales.

Bowhead whales also use their bodies to communicate. Some whales slap the surface of the water with their tails and flippers. Others leap out of the water and fall back, making a big splash. When whales do this, it is called "breaching."

Fun Facts

Bowhead whales have the thickest blubber of any whale. A bowhead whale's layer of blubber is about 17 to 19 inches (about 43 to 48 centimetres) thick. This helps them stay warm in the cold waters of the Arctic.

Bowhead whales live for a very long time. Some bowhead whales still have stone harpoon tips embedded in their blubber. Stone harpoons were used by Inuit hunters long ago, so those whales are thought to be over a hundred years old.

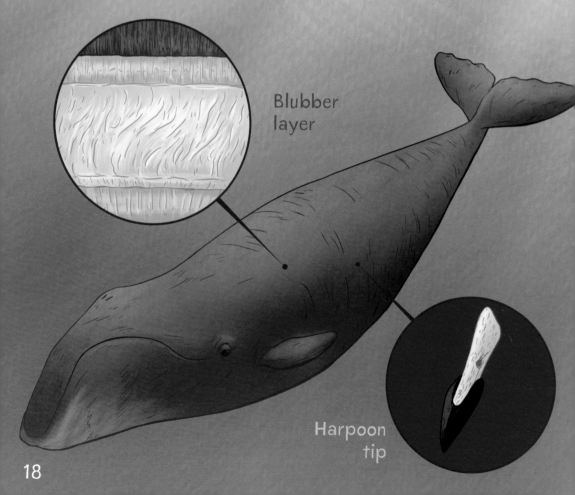

Blubber layer

Harpoon tip

Bowhead whales have the largest mouths of any animal in the world.

Traditional Uses

Inuit have hunted bowhead whales for thousands of years. When Inuit hunters caught a bowhead whale, they used every part of it. Nothing went to waste.

A whale could provide 1 year of building material for an entire camp. Inuit used bowhead whalebones to make frames for their tents.

Qulliq

The blubber from the whale was poured into a lamp called a *"qulliq"* and used for heat and light. Blubber was also used for cooking.

Hunters fed whale meat to their dogs, but the skin was saved for Inuit to eat. The skin had a thick layer of blubber attached to it. Inuit call this *"maktak."* Maktak was placed inside sealskin for aging. When it began to smell, they knew it was ready to eat.

Maktak

Joanasie Karpik is a respected elder from Pangnirtung, Nunavut.

Sho Uehara is an illustrator and cartoonist living in Calgary. He graduated from the Alberta College of Art & Design, where he majored in Character Design & Visual Communications. He has done illustration work for Swerve Calgary and BOOM! Studios, and has completed an independent comic anthology called *Wishless* alongside a group of talented local illustrators. Sho is currently working on self-published comics while doing freelance work.

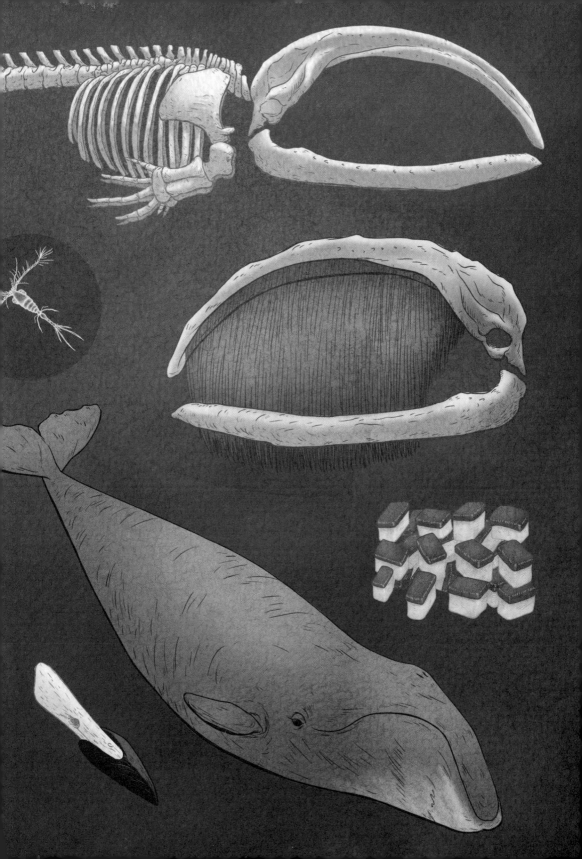